Real People
Real Faith

Amy Grant   Joni Eareckson Tada   Dave Dravecky   Terry Anderson

PHOTO VICTORIA PEARSON

RNS PHOTO/KEVIN MCLAUGHLIN

RNS PHOTO/WIDE WORLD

RNS PHOTO/REUTERS

Loveland, Colorado

*A 4-week course to help senior highers
learn from the examples of modern-day Christians*

by Jennifer Root Wilger

Group®

Real People, *Real* Faith: Amy Grant, Joni Eareckson Tada, Dave Dravecky, Terry Anderson
Copyright © 1994 Group Publishing, Inc.

First Printing

Credits
Edited by Amy Nappa
Cover designed by Diane Whisner
Illustrations by Jan Knudson and Roseanne Buerge

ISBN 1-55945-238-2
Printed in the United States of America

CONTENTS

REAL PEOPLE, *REAL* FAITH: AMY GRANT, JONI EARECKSON TADA, DAVE DRAVECKY, TERRY ANDERSON

"Now even *Superman's* dead! Aren't there any heroes left?"

What do we have to offer teenagers in a world where heroes carry guns, flaunt their bodies, and spew profanity? High school students are looking for someone to emulate, someone who offers guidance for their "modern" problems. Unfortunately, positive role models in current society are few. While Jesus is the only true hero we can encourage students to follow, there *are* contemporary Christians whose examples can bring encouragement to teenagers.

Many of the "modern" problems teenagers face have actually plagued humans for generations. Ever since the first sin, people have had to deal with weakness, unfairness, and disappointment in various forms.

Modern Heroes

Amy Grant

Joni Eareckson Tada

Dave Dravecky

Terry Anderson

These problems have received a "face lift" for the modern age. Salt and light penetrate the darkest corners of the entertainment world through a gospel singer turned Top 40. Years of therapy allow a paraplegic to function effectively in a highly complex society. "Why do bad things happen to good people?" resurfaces in a baseball player with cancer. Hostages from distant nations are confined together in the prison of a common enemy.

It's true— the situations your teenagers face may not be as extreme as the circumstances of the heroes you'll be studying. But the same principles that helped Amy Grant, Joni Eareckson Tada, Dave Dravecky, and Terry Anderson can help your senior highers live out their faith every day.

Amy Grant

"I don't think about success . . . There are so many more important things happening in my life— my nephew's basketball games, my niece's 15th birthday, and her first boyfriend."

These are unusual sentiments from someone like Amy Grant. She's recorded more than 10 albums, the first when she was only 17 years old. She's won Dove and Grammy Awards, toured the world, and had an album that went triple platinum (selling over three million copies). Her music has even reached #1 on the nation's pop music charts.

But while standing in the glare of the limelight and the hype that accompanies national attention, Amy remains focused on what's most important in her life— Jesus.

"My relationship with Jesus," she says, "is the one thing that does surpass the hype. That's a wonderful comfort."

Joni Eareckson Tada

"Wouldn't it be exciting if right now, in front of you, I could be miraculously healed, get up out of my chair and on my feet?"

These words of Joni (pronounced "Johnny") Eareckson Tada only begin to reveal her heart. But before we finish her thoughts, let's take a look at where she's coming from.

On July 30, 1967, Joni Eareckson was an average 17-year-old girl growing up in America. Then, in the span of 60 seconds, her life was changed forever. While swimming with her sister in Chesapeake Bay, Joni suffered a diving accident that left her paralyzed from the neck down.

Yet, Joni's faith in God refused to let that accident ruin her life. She learned how to draw with a pen in her mouth and has become an accomplished artist. She created her own line of Christian greeting cards and even appeared on the *Today Show* to tell her story of faith to millions.

Now, let's finish hearing Joni's thoughts.

"But far more exciting would be the miracle of healing your own soul . . . My body is only a flicker in the time span of forever . . . I wouldn't change my life for anything."

Dave Dravecky

"It began in the back yard with a game of catch . . . w ith my dad," says Dave Dravecky of his baseball career. "It was [in that back yard] . . . I first dreamed of being a big-league pitcher."

Years later, Dave Dravecky had achieved his dream and more. Playing first for the San Diego Padres, then for the San Francisco Giants, he wasn't only a big-league pitcher, he was one of the best. In 1983 he was selected to pitch in the All-Star game. In 1984 he pitched in the World Series. In 1987 he pitched a shutout in the National League championship series.

Then, in 1988, a lump on his pitching arm was diagnosed as cancer. On June 18, 1991, doctors amputated Dave Dravecky's pitching arm as a result of his cancer.

Throughout his ordeal, and now, even though his arm is gone and his baseball career is over, Dave Dravecky remains convinced that God is still in control. His message for others is this: "What do you do when you can't come back? May God give you the grace to put your hand in his— even if you have only one hand to give— and there may you find peace."

Terry Anderson

For Associated Press correspondent Terry Anderson, Saturday mornings were meant for tennis games, not kidnappings. Unfortunately, on Saturday, March 16, 1985, Arab terrorists in Lebanon disagreed. They ambushed Terry on his way home, beginning the first of his 2,455 days of captivity— the longest of any American hostage held in the Middle East.

A glimpse into his captivity reveals barbaric conditions. At times he was chained, blindfolded, and forced to sit on his mattress in his underwear. His diet consisted of cheese and water for breakfast, rice and beans for lunch, and bread and jam for dinner. But perhaps the worst of all was being cut off from family, friends, and the everyday occurrences of the outside world.

But there were bright moments. When guards gave him a Bible, he read it endlessly, memorizing long passages of Scripture. When the Reverend Martin L. Jenco joined Terry in captivity, Terry rediscovered the faith of his youth. Later he said that faith was one of the main things that kept him going.

Upon his release, after nearly seven years imprisonment, Terry surprised reporters at a press conference by saying, "Look, those weren't wasted years, OK? I lived through them, I learned some things from them, and I'll use them, I hope, properly. I've got a whole new life . . . [and] I'm going to enjoy it, God willing."

This four-week course will help your senior highers recognize that other modern Christians have faced situations similar to their own. Use these lessons to teach your teenagers proven techniques for incorporating faith into their daily lives.

American Heroes?

In the World Almanac's 12th annual poll published in 1992, teenagers were asked to list their heroes. Here were their responses:
- SPORTS: Michael Jordan and Jennifer Capriati
- COMEDY: Eddie Murphy and Kirstie Alley
- NEWS: Barbara Walters and Tom Brokaw
- WRITERS: Steven King and Alice Walker
- MUSIC: Mariah Carey and LL Cool J

How would this list be different if the poll were taken today?

COURSE OBJECTIVES

By the end of this course, your students will
- determine to focus on God regardless of what others may think,
- commit to doing their best in spite of their weaknesses,
- explore ways to deal with disappointment in life, and
- learn to trust God when circumstances are out of their control.

HOW TO USE THIS COURSE

ACTIVE LEARNING

Think back on an important lesson you've learned in life. Did you learn it from reading about it? from hearing about it? from something you experienced? Chances are, the most important lessons you've learned came from something you experienced. That's what active learning is—learning by doing. And active learning is a key element in Group's Active Bible Curriculum®.

Active learning leads students in doing things that help them understand important principles, messages, and ideas. It's a discovery process that helps kids internalize what they learn.

Each lesson section in Group's Active Bible Curriculum plays an important part in active learning:

The **Opener** involves kids in the topic in fun and unusual ways.

The **Action and Reflection** includes an experience designed to evoke specific feelings in the students. This section also processes those feelings through "How did you feel?" questions and applies the message to situations kids face.

The **Bible Application** actively connects the topic with the Bible. It helps kids see how the Bible is relevant to the situations they face.

The **Commitment** helps students internalize the Bible's message and commit to making changes in their lives.

The **Closing** funnels the lesson's message into a time of creative reflection and prayer.

When you put all the sections together, you get a lesson that's fun to teach. And kids get messages they'll remember.

BEFORE THE 4-WEEK SESSION

● Read the Introduction, the Course Objectives, and This Course at a Glance.

● Decide how you'll publicize the course using the clip art on the Publicity Page (p. 11). Prepare fliers, newsletter articles and posters as needed.

● Look at the Bonus Ideas (p. 50) and decide which ones you'll use.

• Read the opening statements, Objectives, and Bible Basis for the lesson. The Bible Basis shows how specific passages relate to senior highers today.

• Choose which Opener and Closing options to use. Each is appropriate for a different kind of group.

• Gather necessary supplies from This Lesson at a Glance.

• Read each section of the lesson. Adjust where necessary for your class size and meeting room.

• The approximate minutes listed give you an idea of how long each activity will take. Each lesson is designed to take 35 to 60 minutes. Shorten or lengthen activities as needed to fit your group.

• If you see you're going to have extra time, do an activity or two from the "If You Still Have Time . . . " box or from the Bonus Ideas (p. 50).

• Dive into the activities with the kids. Don't be a spectator. The lesson will be more successful and rewarding to both you and your students.

• Though some kids may at first think certain activities are "silly," they'll enjoy them and they'll remember the messages from these activities long after the lesson is over. As one Active Bible Curriculum user has said, "I can ask the kids questions about a lesson I did three weeks ago and they actually remember what I taught!" And that's the whole idea of teaching . . . isn't it?

Have fun with the activities you lead. Remember, it is Jesus who encourages us to become "like little children." Besides, how often do your kids get *permission* to express their childlike qualities?

• The answers given after discussion questions are responses your students *might* give. They aren't the only answers or the "right" answers. If needed, use them to spark discussion. Kids won't always say what you wish they'd say. That's why some of the responses given are negative or controversial. If someone responds negatively, don't be shocked. Accept the person and use the opportunity to explore other angles of the issue.

THIS COURSE AT A GLANCE

Before you dive into the lessons, familiarize yourself with each lesson aim. Then read the Scripture passages.
- Study them as a background to the lessons.
- Use them as a basis for your personal devotions.
- Think about how they relate to kids' circumstances today.

LESSON 1: LIFE IN THE LIMELIGHT: AMY GRANT

Lesson Aim: To help senior highers express their Christian faith in a non-Christian world.

Bible Basis: Matthew 5:13-16; Philippians 1:27-28a; 2:14-16a.

LESSON 2: HELP FOR THE HELPLESS: JONI EARECKSON TADA

Lesson Aim: To help senior highers rely on God's power when they feel weak.

Bible Basis: Exodus 3:1-12; 4:10-17; Jeremiah 1:4-10, 17-19; Ruth 2:1-3; Deuteronomy 24:19-22.

LESSON 3: IN PURSUIT OF THE DREAM: DAVE DRAVECKY

Lesson Aim: To help senior highers identify their dreams and look to God for guidance in pursuing those dreams.

Bible Basis: Job 8:4-6; 11:14; 15:11-13; Romans 5:1-5.

LESSON 4: OUT OF CONTROL: TERRY ANDERSON

Lesson Aim: To help senior highers trust God when their lives seem out of control.

Bible Basis: Daniel 1:1-16; 2:1-23, 48-49; 3:4-30; 6:1-28; Romans 8:28-31.

PUBLICITY PAGE

Grab your senior highers' attention! Photocopy this page, and then cut and paste the clip art of your choice in your church bulletin or newsletter to advertise this course on modern heroes of the faith. Or photocopy and use the ready-made flier as a bulletin insert. Permission to photocopy this clip art is granted for local church use.

Splash the clip art on posters, fliers, or even postcards! Just add the vital details: the date and time the course begins and where you'll meet.

It's that simple.

 **DAVE DRAVECKY**

 Joni Eareckson Tada

 *Amy Grant*

 Terry Anderson

Real People Real Faith

Amy Grant Joni Eareckson Tada Dave Dravecky Terry Anderson

DAVE DRAVECKY **Joni Eareckson Tada**

Amy Grant **Terry Anderson**

A 4-week high school course on modern heroes of the Christian faith

Come to _____

On _____

At _____

Come learn how today's heroes deal with issues of the Christian faith.

LIFE IN THE LIMELIGHT: AMY GRANT

Due to her Top 40 success, Amy Grant and her music have become well-known to Christians and non-Christians alike. As a result, people everywhere are watching closely to see whether Amy will live up to the Christian values she professes.

Like Amy Grant, Christian teenagers are also being watched by others. Friends, family, and teachers keep a close eye on kids to see if their lives match their beliefs. By using Amy Grant as an example, this lesson will help teenagers deal positively with the "Christian limelight."

To help senior highers express their Christian faith in a non-Christian world.

LESSON AIM

Students will
- **examine how the limelight can affect their faith,**
- **see how helpful light is to those in darkness, and**
- **prepare answers for those who challenge their relationships with non-Christians.**

OBJECTIVES

Look up the following verses. Then read the background paragraphs to see how the passage relates to your senior highers.

In **Matthew 5:13-16**, Jesus teaches his disciples to be salt and light to the world.

BIBLE BASIS
MATTHEW 5:13-16

By using metaphors of salt and light, Jesus encourages his disciples to take the good news they've heard into the world. There, their acts of devotion to God will be noticed and imitated.

Your students may feel afraid or unprepared to share their faith with non-Christian friends. Although they realize others are watching them, they may de-emphasize or even deny their Christian beliefs when the pressure's on. Kids need encouragement to live a consistently Christian lifestyle. Then they'll also become salt and light to the world.

THIS LESSON AT A GLANCE

Section	Minutes	What Students Will Do	Supplies
Opener (Option 1)	5 to 10	**A Different Drum**—Compare an Amy Grant song to a secular Top 40 song.	*Heart in Motion* and *Whitney Houston* cassettes, cassette player, pencils, paper
(Option 2)		**Limelight**—Experience life in the limelight by answering questions about themselves.	Flashlight
Action and Reflection	10 to 15	**Popular?**—Explore what it means to be popular and how popularity can affect their faith.	Prepared slips of paper
Bible Application	15 to 20	**Spread a Little Light**—Try to find something in a dark room.	Three dictionaries, paper bags, matchbook, matches, candle, flashlight, Bibles
Commitment	5 to 10	**The Best Defense**—Write letters to encourage one another in their Christian lives.	Paper, pencils
Closing (Option 1)	up to 5	**Shining Examples**—Share ways to shine their Christian lights this week.	Bibles
(Option 2)		**Hope Set High**—Listen to an Amy Grant song and share what their legacies could be.	*Heart in Motion* cassette, cassette player

The Lesson

☐ OPTION 1: A DIFFERENT DRUM

Distribute pencils and paper.

Say: **I'm going to play two songs. As you listen to each song, write down two or three words to describe how that song makes you feel.**

Play "Every Heartbeat" from Amy Grant's *Heart in Motion* cassette. After you've played the song, have kids form pairs and discuss their feelings about the song with their partners. Have partners discuss the following questions:

● **What's this song about?** (Love; staying together when it's hard; I'm not sure.)

● **How did you feel as you listened to this song?** (Good, I liked it; hopeful; depressed, because I don't have a boyfriend or girlfriend.)

Say: **I want you to keep the message of this song in mind as I play the next one. See if you notice anything different about the messages of the two songs.**

Play "Saving All My Love" from Whitney Houston's *Whitney Houston* album. Remember to have students write a few words about how the song makes them feel. Then have partners discuss their feelings about the song.

Bring the group together and ask:

● **What is this song about?** (Love; relationships; having an affair.)

● **How is this song different from the first song?** (It's by a different artist; it's more about sex than love; it doesn't have a positive view of love.)

● **What did you think as I played this song?** (I liked it; I was disappointed in the words; I didn't like the message.)

● **Should a Christian artist perform a song like this one? Why or why not?** (No, it promotes unfaithfulness; yes, maybe a Christian artist could witness to non-Christians at concerts; I don't know.)

● **Should a Christian artist perform the first song we heard? Why or why not?** (No, it sounds too much like other popular music; yes, the message is better; Christian artists can show their faith by living Christian lifestyles.)

Say: **Amy Grant recorded her first album when she was 17 and became popular singing songs with a Christian message. She's been even more in the limelight in the past few years because of her decision to perform Top-40-style music. Some Christians accuse her of abandoning her faith. Others applaud her for living a lifestyle that makes a positive statement about her faith to her non-Christian listeners. Like Amy Grant, each one of us must**

OPENER
(5 to 10 minutes)

be prepared to answer to God for the lifestyle choices we make, regardless of what others may think or say. Today's lesson will help us see that, as Christians, we're *all* in the limelight.

☐ OPTION 2: LIMELIGHT

Turn off the lights in the room. Shine a flashlight against a wall to create a spotlight. Ask for a volunteer to stand "in the limelight."

Say: **For the next 30 seconds, we're all going to ask our volunteer questions about himself** (or herself). **You may ask anything you want, but our volunteer can say "pass" if he** (or she) **doesn't want to answer. Audience, try to fit in as many questions as you can.**

Have as many volunteers experience "the limelight" as time allows.

Turn on the lights and say:

● **Describe how you felt when you were in the limelight.** (Important; scared; on the spot.)

● **How did you feel when you rejoined the audience?** (Relieved; glad; I tried not to ask embarrassing questions.)

● **What was your reaction if you had to be in the audience for the whole activity?** (Jealous; glad I wasn't put on the spot.)

● **How is being in the audience for the whole activity like living your Christian faith in the world?** (Sometimes you can try to hide your faith; it's easier to be "one of the crowd.")

● **How is this activity like the situations a popular singer like Amy Grant might face?** (Everyone wants to know about her personal life now that she's popular; sometimes she might choose not to answer a question if she thinks it's too personal.)

● **How is being in the limelight in this game like living your Christian faith in the world?** (You stand out; everyone's watching you; people are interested in the things you do.)

Say: **Although we may not realize it, each of us is in the limelight every day. As Christians, the world is constantly watching us to see if we'll be true to what we say we believe. Today we'll be studying the example of Amy Grant to see how we can stay focused on Jesus, no matter what others may say.**

Teacher Tip

If students are unfamiliar with Amy Grant, take a moment to read aloud the biographical information about her in the introduction to this course (p. 5).

ACTION AND REFLECTION
(10 to 15 minutes)

POPULAR?

Before the meeting, cut a slip of paper for each student. On half of the slips write "popular" and on the other half write "unpopular." Give each student a slip of paper. Tell kids not to reveal whether they're "popular" or "unpopular" until the end of the activity.

Say: **You've each been given a slip of paper that says whether you're popular or unpopular. If you're popular, you may associate only with other popular people. If you're unpopular, you may associate only with other unpopular people. You have five minutes to find the others in your group. However, you can't say, "I'm popular," or "I'm unpopular." To decide whether someone is popular or unpopular, you must ask questions such as "What do you do for fun?" or "What kind of music do you listen to?" Depending on the answers, you have to determine whether that person is popular or not.**

Give kids about five minutes to decide who they think is popular and unpopular. Then call the group back together. Have students reveal their identities, then have popular students pair up with unpopular students. Ask the following questions and have students discuss their answers with their partners.

- **How did you react when you discovered you were popular?** (I felt relieved, glad; accepted.)

- **What did you think when you discovered you were unpopular?** (I thought this was a stupid game; I felt cheated; glad it was only a game.)

- **What defines popularity?** (Popular people have lots of friends; popular people can do whatever they want.)

- **Why do people think it's important to be popular?** (Because it makes you feel like you're worth something; it saves you from being lonely.)

- **What would you be willing to do to be popular? to stay popular? Why?** (I'd be willing to hang out with people who are snobs; I'd be willing to wear the right kind of clothes; I'd listen to music I didn't even like.)

- **Does the desire to be popular affect your faith? Why or why not?** (Yes, sometimes being a Christian isn't too popular at school; I don't let anyone know I'm a Christian; no, my friends know I'm a Christian, and they still like me; I have only Christian friends.)

- **How do you think a popular artist like Amy Grant feels as she tries to write and perform songs everyone will like while being a Christian example?** (Like it's too stressful; tempted to sing only for Christians; like it's a great way to show others what she believes.)

- **How are Amy Grant's circumstances like the popularity activity?** (She's trying to get everyone to like her music; she has to find people who will buy her music; she doesn't want to offend Christians and non-Christians.)

Invite students to share what they discussed with their partners.

Say: **Artists like Amy Grant often find themselves in situations in which they might be tempted to compromise**

Teacher Tip

Kids who really feel unpopular may have difficulty processing this activity. If kids open up about their feelings, take time away from the regular lesson to help kids process why they feel unpopular. Help them see that God sees each of us as valuable, no matter what the world sees.

their faith in order to stay popular. Like Amy Grant, every Christian struggles to live a Christian lifestyle in a non-Christian environment. Let's see what the Bible has to say about this.

BIBLE APPLICATION

(15 to 20 minutes)

SPREAD A LITTLE LIGHT

Before the meeting, prepare three paper bags. In the first, put a matchbook containing only one match. In the second, place matches and a candle, and in the third, a flashlight. Hide three dictionaries in separate places in the room.

Form three groups.

Say: **There are three dictionaries hidden in this room. Each group needs to find one and look up the definition of "light." To make the hunt more challenging, I'm going to turn out the lights. Use whatever is in your group's bag to help you in your search.**

Give each group one of the bags and turn out the lights. It's important to darken the room as much as possible so kids will need to use the flashlight, matches, and candle. If necessary, move this activity to a different room that can easily be darkened.

Allow several minutes for groups to search the room. Then turn on the lights and call everyone together, whether or not groups have found their dictionaries.

If any group found a hidden dictionary, ask that group to read the definition of "light" aloud. Have any groups not finding the dictionaries define "light" in their own words.

Ask:

● **How did you react when you discovered what was in your paper bag?** (Glad, we just turned on the flashlight and went to work; annoyed, we couldn't see anything when our match went out; at first I was glad to have our candle, but then it blew out.)

● **What's so important about light?** (You can't see without it; it leads you; it keeps you from tripping in the dark.)

● **What does light have to do with being an example to others?** (What we do and say can guide others; just as light shows us obstacles, our example can help keep others from making mistakes.)

Say: **Let's see what the Bible has to say about light.**

Have groups read Matthew 5:13-16 and Philippians 2:14-16a together. After they've read the Scriptures, have group members discuss the following questions and share their answers with the class.

● **Think about the three kinds of light we used in the last activity. What kind of light do you shine in the world around you? Explain.** (My light is like a candle because sometimes I'm afraid it will get blown out; my light is like a flashlight because it's powered by another source.)

● **What obstacles keep you from shining your light in the world?** (I'm afraid my friends will think I'm strange if I tell them I'm a Christian; I don't know how to explain my faith to my friends.)

● **How can you make your light stronger and brighter?** (I could get together with other Christians in my school; I could learn more by reading the Bible every day; I could trust God more and not worry about what others think.)

Turn out the lights and light the candle. Set it in the middle of the room. Ask:

● **What good is one small light?** (It's better than total darkness; even a little light can show you the way; it can still show you obstacles.)

● **How is someone like Amy Grant a light to others?** (She shows people that Christians are real people, not perfect saints; people can get a positive message from her music; through her example others can learn more about what a Christian is.)

● **How can Amy Grant's example encourage you to be a brighter light?** (If she can stand up for what she believes in an industry filled with sex and violence, I can certainly stand up for what I believe at school; you can tell what she believes by her life and music, and I want people to know me that way, too.)

Say: **If you're living a Christian lifestyle, your friends will definitely notice. You might even feel like you're in the spotlight because everyone watches what you do and say. Actually, you *are* the spotlight! God is using *you* to light up the dark corners of the world.**

Blow out the candle and turn on the lights.

THE BEST DEFENSE

Say: **Some Christians say Amy Grant should sing only Christian music or she should let her music be played only on Christian radio stations. Here's what two people wrote defending what Amy Grant does.**

Read the following letters:

How come so many people point their fingers at Amy Grant for becoming "worldly" when they probably sit next to people at school or live next door to neighbors who have never heard them say, "Jesus loves you?"

A Christian doctor can't decide to treat only Christian patients, and a Christian teacher has every right to teach in a public school. A Christian singer like Amy Grant should be allowed to minister and show love to non-Christians as well as Christians. We should stop trying to judge Amy Grant. Only God should judge what kind of ministry she should or shouldn't have.

COMMITMENT
(5 to 10 minutes)

After you've read the letters, distribute pencils and paper.

Say: **Find a partner and talk about the ways you each choose to live out your Christian faith. Then write a letter like the ones I read, defending your partner's Christian lifestyle choices.**

For example, if your partner hangs around with a group of non-Christian friends at school, your letter might say, "I know sometimes people at church get on your case for your choice of friends. But I know you're committed to Christ and you're always ready to stand up for that belief. I admire you for proudly admitting you're a Christian."

Give kids several minutes to write and share their letters with their partners. Encourage kids each to keep their partner's letter where they'll be able to find it easily when they feel discouraged about their Christian walk.

Table Talk

The "Table Talk" activity in this course helps senior highers talk with their parents about modern heroes whose examples they can follow.

If you choose to use the "Table Talk" activity, this is a good time to show students the "Table Talk" handout (p. 22). Ask them to spend time with their parents completing it.

Before kids leave, give them each the "Table Talk" handout to take home, or tell them you'll be sending it to their parents. Tell kids to be prepared to report on their experiences with the handout.

Or use the "Table Talk" idea found in the Bonus Ideas (p. 51) for a meeting based on the handout.

CLOSING
(up to 5 minutes)

☐ OPTION 1: SHINING EXAMPLES

Ask one volunteer to read Philippians 1:27-28a and another to read 1 Timothy 4:12.

Say: **Think of one way you can shine Christ's light in your relationships with non-Christians this week. For example, you might want to pray silently before you eat your lunch or commit to bringing a friend to church next week.**

Turn out the lights and pass around a lit candle. As each student takes the candle have him or her share his or her idea. After all kids have shared, read John 8:12.

Close in prayer, asking God to help kids shine Christ's light this week.

☐ OPTION 2: HOPE SET HIGH

Say: **In an interview with Contemporary Christian Music magazine, Amy Grant was asked the question, "If your career would end today, what would you want your** legacy to be?" Her answer was simple and to the point: "She was real and honest, and she loved God. And that God used her in spite of herself."

Ask:

● **What would you want your legacy to be?** (Answers will vary.)

Close by playing "Hope Set High" from Amy Grant's *Heart in Motion* cassette.

If You Still Have Time . . .

Lips in Motion—Form groups of no more than three. Have each group pick their favorite song from Amy Grant's *Heart in Motion* cassette and lip-sync that song to the class.

Bright Ideas—Have kids think of the ways they can "shine their lights" this week. What are ways group members can be supportive of one another in this? ways the church can be supportive?

Table Talk

To the Parent: We're involved in a senior high course at church called *Real People*, Real *Faith: Amy Grant, Joni Eareckson Tada, Dave Dravecky, Terry Anderson*. Students are learning how modern-day Christians have faced tough issues kids face every day. We'd like you and your teenager to spend some time discussing this important topic. Use this "Table Talk" page to help you do that.

Parent
- Think back to your high school years. Who were your heroes? Why?
- Who are some people you look up to today? Why?
- What are ways you live out your Christian faith in your job or career?
- Relate an incident from your life when God worked through you in spite of your weaknesses.
- What do you do when you feel like circumstances are out of your control? How can God help?

Senior higher
- What qualities do you look for in a hero? Why?
- Who are your heroes? Are they the same now as when you were younger? Explain.
- Are there any situations in your life that you feel are out of your control? How can your parent help you in this area?
- What's one dream you'd like to realize in the next 10 years?
- Share a specific way you'd like to shine Christ's light at school this week.

Parent and senior higher
Decide whether you agree or disagree with the following statements. Explain your answers.
- Living the Christian faith is sometimes embarrassing.
- If we rely on God, he'll take away all our weaknesses.
- Even our hopes and dreams can glorify God.
- God sometimes takes control away from us to make us more trusting.

Read 2 Corinthians 12:9-10 together. What are your weaknesses? How can God's grace work through them? How can the members of your family complement each other's strengths and weaknesses?

Amy Grant   Joni Eareckson Tada   Dave Dravecky   Terry Anderson

HELP FOR THE HELPLESS: JONI EARECKSON TADA

In one swift moment, Joni Eareckson had her hopes and dreams dashed as her head pounded the ocean floor. One second she was a normal, active teenager. The next, a paralytic. Yet in spite of her grave injuries, Joni battled back. Today Joni Eareckson Tada is happily married and helping to ease others' suffering through her ministry, "Joni and Friends." This lesson will help your teenagers put their weaknesses into perspective by taking a look at life from a disabled person's point of view.

To help senior highers rely on God's power when they feel weak.

LESSON AIM

Students will
- experience being disabled,
- learn that God can work through their weaknesses, and
- compare their hardships to those of various biblical characters.

OBJECTIVES

Look up the following Scriptures. Then read the background paragraphs to see how the passages relate to your senior highers.

Exodus 3:1-12 and **4:10-17** record Moses' call to lead God's people to freedom.

The Bible tells us Moses was not a skilled speaker. Perhaps he even had a stutter. But whatever its nature, Moses' speech impediment didn't stop him from accomplishing God's purpose.

Like Moses, teenagers often feel shy about their speaking abilities. They may want to tell their friends about Christ but aren't sure they'll know what to say. Use the example of Moses to help your teenagers realize God can give them the words their friends need to hear.

Jeremiah 1:4-10, 17-19 describes Jeremiah's call to be a prophet.

Tradition tells us Jeremiah was probably a teenager when God called him. At first he protested, saying he was too young to be a prophet. But as soon as he was assured of God's protection, he jumped at the opportunity to serve God. Jeremiah grew up to become one of God's most faithful prophets. He persevered in his mission, even when it made him unpopular.

Many teenagers identify with Jeremiah because they share his disability—youth. They want to serve God but don't think their efforts will be taken seriously. Jeremiah's example will help teenagers realize that, by using their gifts, they can make valuable contributions to the lives of others.

Deuteronomy 24:19-22 provides the background for **Ruth 2:1-3**. **Ruth 2:1-3** tells how Ruth had to glean in the fields to get enough food to eat.

From the start, Ruth had two strikes against her: She was a widow and a foreigner. But God watched over Ruth in her weakness. Ruth not only found food, she also found a new husband and became part of a family of faith.

In today's mobile society, most teenagers have probably had to pick up and leave home at least once. Or perhaps they've had friends who moved, leaving them lonely. Use the example of Ruth to teach your teenagers that God can give them a fresh start at any time in their lives.

Section	Minutes	What Students Will Do	Supplies
Opener (Option 1) (Option 2)	5 to 10	**Hidden Talents**—Guess one another's hidden talents. **I Can Do It Myself!**—Arrange chairs while limited by physical disabilities.	Pencils, paper, tape
Action and Reflection	10 to 15	**A Humbling Experience**—Draw and write using markers in their mouths.	Markers, newsprint
Bible Application	15 to 20	**Here's the Catch**—Learn about Bible characters God used in spite of their weaknesses.	Bibles, "The Catch" handouts (p. 31)
Commitment	5 to 10	**The Great Frame-Up**—Affirm one another's strengths.	
Closing (Option 1) (Option 2)	up to 5	**What Holds You Back?**—Compare their hardships to hardships Jesus experienced. **Tapping Into God's Power**—Affirm God's power in one another.	Bibles Bible

The Lesson

☐ OPTION 1: HIDDEN TALENTS

Pass out pencils and paper.

Say: **Think of a hidden talent you have that not many people know about. Perhaps you can wiggle your ears or pick things up with your toes. Take a few minutes to write or draw your hidden talent. Don't put your name on it!**

As students are drawing their hidden talents, draw a simple picture of a mouth holding a paintbrush to represent Joni Eareckson Tada.

Gather all papers and tape them to the wall. Have kids guess which talent goes with which person. As kids guess each person's talent, have that person demonstrate his or her hidden ability. After everyone's talents have been guessed, have kids guess what your drawing represents. Explain the drawing and introduce kids to Joni Eareckson Tada.

Say: **Joni** (pronounced "Johnny") **Eareckson Tada is a talented artist by any standard. Her talent is exceptional when you consider she was injured in a diving accident when she was a teenager. As a result, she is paralyzed**

OPENER
(5 to 10 minutes)

from the neck down. In spite of the obstacles she faces each day, Joni continues to live a fulfilling life. Today we'll explore ways to follow Joni's example in dealing with the obstacles we face.

☐ OPTION 2: I CAN DO IT MYSELF!

Before class, make sure none of the chairs are set up.

As students arrive, assign each of them one of the following disabilities: blindness, inability to use writing hand, inability to use both hands, or inability to use feet. (Several students may have the same disability.) After you've assigned students disabilities, ask them all to help you place the chairs in a circle. Emphasize that everyone must help. After several minutes, encourage students to pool their abilities to complete the task.

After the chairs are arranged, sit in the circle and ask:

● **What was your reaction when you found out about your disability? Explain.** (Glad I wasn't totally disabled; upset I couldn't do anything.)

● **Describe how you felt when I asked you to move the chairs.** (Hopeless; challenged; I didn't think I could be of any help.)

● **How did you feel when I said you could help each other? Explain.** (Encouraged, because it got a little easier; relieved to know I didn't have to move the chair myself; happy, because it was more fun.)

● **When have you felt similar emotions about an obstacle you faced in life?** (When I tried out for a sports team; when I moved to a new school and had to make friends; when I enrolled in advanced English.)

Say: **Sometimes when we're facing a big obstacle, it's hard to imagine things could get any worse. Today we're going to study the example of Joni Eareckson Tada, a paralyzed Christian artist who paints with a brush in her teeth. By focusing on Joni's example, we'll learn new ways to overcome the obstacles we face each day.**

Teacher Tip

If students are unfamiliar with Joni Eareckson Tada, take a moment to read aloud the biographical information about her in the introduction to this course (p. 5).

Table Talk Follow-Up

If you sent the "Table Talk" handout (p. 22) to parents last week, discuss students' reactions to the activity. Ask volunteers to share what they learned from the discussion with their parents.

A HUMBLING EXPERIENCE

Ask an adult volunteer or a student to act as a judge for the following activity.

Give each person a sheet of newsprint and a marker.

Say: **To help us understand Joni's disability better, we're going to draw with our mouths. Remember, if you're Joni, you can't use your arms or hands because they're paralyzed. Keep your hands behind your backs at all times. Start by drawing geometric shapes like circles and squares.**

Help kids position the markers in their mouths and let them practice mouth drawing on the newsprint.

After one or two minutes, call time. Invite students to view one another's mouth drawings. Then introduce your judge. Have students reposition their markers in their mouths and ask them to write their names in cursive on their papers.

When students have finished, lead your judge around to examine students' work. Prepare your judge before class with comments like "How can I judge something I can't even read?" and "I thought this was a high school class, but these look like they were done by kindergartners." Ignore all students' protests about having to write with their mouths.

After your judge has commented on each student's work, ask:

● **Was it easy or hard to draw using a marker in your mouth? Explain.** (It was easy once I got the hang of it; it was hard because the marker kept slipping; it hurt my teeth.)

● **Was it easier to draw the first time or the second time? Why?** (The first time was easier because shapes are simple; the second time was easier because I can write better than I can draw.)

● **How do you think Joni Eareckson Tada felt when she first started drawing with a marker in her mouth?** (Embarrassed because she looked funny; discouraged because no one could read what she wrote.)

● **How did you feel as your drawings were judged?** (Cheated, because I worked really hard; proud, because I could read my name.)

● **How was having your drawings judged just now like judging a disabled person?** (The judge didn't care that I was disabled; disabled people do the best they can, and we judge them anyway; sometimes we act like disabled people can't do anything for themselves.)

Say: **It's easy to judge a person with a physical disability like paralysis because we can see the difficulties that person must face. What kinds of problems can result from other disabilities? Explain.** (Not being able to pay attention in school because of a learning

Teacher Tip

Felt-tip markers work best for this activity because they don't require a lot of pressure to write. Avoid using pencils as they could splinter in students' mouths.

disability; losing friends because of a bad temper; being left out of activities because of finances.)

● **How do you think God judges disabled people?** (God judges everyone the same; God only expects us to do our best.)

Say: **Even those in perfect physical health must face disabilities in life. We may struggle to succeed in school or have difficulty making friends. We may have to scrimp and save to afford a college education. But just as God has used Joni, God can use us in spite of our disabilities. Let's look at disabilities people in the Bible faced and see how God used them.**

HERE'S THE CATCH

Photocopy "The Catch" handout (p. 31). Make enough copies so each group will have one character sketch.

Form groups of no more than four. Give each group a copy of one character sketch from "The Catch" handout.

Say: **You'll have five minutes to come up with a short skit about your Bible character to present to the class. Use the ideas on the handout to get you started. As you read about your character, think about how "the catch" relates to your character's story. Be sure to incorporate the catch into your presentation.**

After about five minutes, call the groups back together. Have students present their skits.

Ask:

● **What was going on inside you as you presented your skits with the catch?** (I felt silly walking around on my knees; I felt dumb presenting a skit to the wall.)

● **How did the catch relate to your characters?** (Moses had trouble speaking; Jeremiah might have been short because he was young; Ruth left her home.)

● **How do you think your characters felt in the situations they faced?** (Scared; glad that God loved them in spite of their weaknesses.)

● **How would you feel if you were in your character's situation? Explain.** (If I were Ruth, I'd feel pretty desperate because I had no friends to turn to; if I were Jeremiah, I'd wonder if people would believe me when I told them about the voices I heard.)

● **Why do you think God would choose to use people with weaknesses when he could have picked people who were strong?** (God wants people to have to trust him; God's power would show up more by using weak people.)

● **How is the catch in your skit like the real disabilities you face in life?** (I have to go on in spite of a disability; sometimes I'm embarrassed by my disabilities.)

● **What can you do this week to follow the example of Joni Eareckson Tada and the Bible characters we've just**

BIBLE APPLICATION
(15 to 20 minutes)

Teacher Tip

If you have more than three groups, assign specific sections of the sketches to be acted out. For example, have one "Moses" group do the first suggested skit and the other "Moses" group do the second skit.

learned about? (Pray that God will help me with my weaknesses; don't sit around complaining about my problems; find a creative way around my problem.)

Say: **It's comforting to know we aren't the first or only people with disabilities who have decided to follow God. God can turn our disabilities to his advantage if we let him.**

THE GREAT FRAME-UP

Have kids lie on the floor and form a square. Ask one student to sit in the center of the square. (If your class has more than eight members, form two squares.)

Say: **As Joni Eareckson Tada was trying to make sense of her paralysis, a friend shared this illustration with her: "Joni, your body—in the chair—is only the frame for God's portrait of you. Y'know, people don't go to an art gallery to admire frames. Their focus is on the quality and character of the painting."**

God created Joni, and each person here, to be special and unique. No matter how severe we may think our disabilities are, God can still use us. We've formed a human frame around (name of person in the center). **Let's each name one way we think God can use** (name of person).

After you've gone around the square, have the center person replace someone else in the human frame. Continue the activity until you've affirmed each student.

☐ OPTION 1: WHAT HOLDS YOU BACK?

Have kids look up Hebrews 4:14-16. Ask a volunteer to read the passage aloud. Form pairs and read the following questions, pausing after each one to allow students to share their answers.

● **What disabilities do you face?** (I want to go to a good college, but I don't know if my family will be able to afford it; my temper gets me into trouble; I judge people before I know enough about them.)

● **What similar disabilities did Jesus face in his life on earth?** (People might have thought Jesus was crazy because he said he was God; Jesus was limited by his human body.)

● **How can you let Jesus help you overcome your disabilities?** (Follow his example and treat others the way I want to be treated; pray and ask Jesus to help me be strong.)

Say: **Disabilities can sometimes make us feel weak, but Jesus understands our weaknesses and can help us overcome them.**

Have partners pray for each other, asking God for help overcoming the obstacles they've discussed.

COMMITMENT
(5 to 10 minutes)

CLOSING
(up to 5 minutes)

OPTION 2: TAPPING INTO GOD'S POWER

Have kids sit in a circle and clasp their hands behind their backs. Read 2 Corinthians 12:9-10 aloud, then sit down and join the circle.

Start the following affirmation by saying to the person on your right: (Name), **God's power is made perfect in you.** Tap the person's shoulder with your head to signify "pass it on."

When each person has been affirmed, close in prayer, asking God to use kids in spite of their weaknesses.

If You Still Have Time . . .

Let Me Help—Brainstorm a list of tasks students can do for disabled or elderly people in your church or neighborhood. Commit to doing one project as a class or list tasks on index cards and keep them in a file students can refer to whenever they want to help.

I'm So Great Because . . . I'm Not!—Form pairs. Have one partner relate a few of his or her weaknesses and the other suggest ways God can work through those weaknesses. These can be serious or funny. For example, a student might say, "I'm terrible at algebra," and his or her partner could reply, "Maybe God will use you to share your faith with your algebra teacher during all the tutoring sessions you'll have." Then have partners switch roles and repeat the activity.

THE CATCH

Read Exodus 3:1-12; 4:10-17. Then present one of the following situations to the class.

● If Moses were alive today, he'd probably be a great political leader. Pretend you're the members of Moses' campaign team having a strategy meeting to get him elected.

● When Moses led the people in the desert he seemed to have a knack for finding water. If Moses were alive today, he'd probably be an expert well driller. Pretend you've gone out with Moses on an excavation.

● Moses received the first law directly from God. If Moses were alive today, he'd probably be a Supreme Court justice. Pretend you're the lawyers and clients presenting a case before him.

THE CATCH: You must all speak with a stutter!

Moses

Jeremiah

Read Jeremiah 1:4-10, 17-19. Then present one of the following situations to the class.

● If Jeremiah were alive today, he'd probably preach incredible sermons. Pretend you're members of the church worship team planning this week's service with Jeremiah.

● Several times, God asked Jeremiah to perform strange actions as signs of things God was about to do. Pretend you're about to observe one of these strange "sign-acts." (For ideas, check out Jeremiah 13 or 19.)

● God asked Jeremiah to write his message on a scroll. Jeremiah entrusted this task to Baruch, his scribe. Pretend you're Jeremiah and Baruch in a dictation session. (For ideas, check out Jeremiah 36 and 45.)

THE CATCH: You must give your entire performance on your knees.

Read Deuteronomy 24:19-22 and Ruth 2:1-3. Then present one of the following situations to the class.

● If Ruth were alive today, she might be the head of a homeless shelter. Pretend your group is working in the shelter's soup kitchen.

● The book of Ruth tells us that Ruth cried twice as she tried to say goodbye to her mother-in-law. Pretend you're members of Ruth's family leaving a family reunion.

THE CATCH: You must give your entire performance with your backs to the audience.

Ruth

IN PURSUIT OF THE DREAM: DAVE DRAVECKY

Since the age of 7, Dave Dravecky had dreamed of playing professional baseball. How excited he was to be drafted by the Pittsburgh Pirates straight out of college! His dream was launched, and he worked diligently for the next four years to make it to the majors. Dave Dravecky was sailing high on the crest of his dream— so high, he failed to notice the small lump on his arm that would eventually become cancerous and force his retirement from baseball.

Like Dave Dravecky, kids often just assume they'll be able to realize their dreams. They're young and invincible, and they dream big. They don't realize dreams are fragile. Use Dave Dravecky's example to teach kids that God can bring good out of shattered dreams.

LESSON AIM

To help senior highers identify their dreams and look to God for guidance in pursuing those dreams.

OBJECTIVES

Students will
- chase after a team goal,
- examine Job's response to suffering, and
- encourage others to pursue God's dreams as well as their own.

Look up the following Scriptures. Then read the background paragraphs to see how the passages relate to your senior highers.

Job 8:4-6; 11:14; and **15:11-13** record the advice of Job's three friends.

After lashing out at God and cursing the day of his birth, Job enters into dialogue with his friends about his suffering. His three friends offer him standard answers, none of which comforts Job.

Teenagers have many questions about the suffering and disappointment they face in life. Why me? Did I do something wrong? Is God mad at me? Use the example of Job to show teenagers that it's OK to ask questions when they encounter troubles or disappointments.

Romans 5:1-5 tells the good things that can result from troubles.

In these five verses, Paul details a chain of events that may seem to start badly, but becomes more and more hopeful over time. Troubles produce patience, which produces character, which produces hope, which leads us to believe in and accept the comfort of God's Holy Spirit.

Teenagers and adults alike often have trouble seeing to the end of this chain reaction. It's easy for kids to get so bogged down in a particular trouble that they forget about God altogether. These verses will remind kids that the same God that can guide their dreams to completion will be there to comfort them during disappointing times.

Section	Minutes	What Students Will Do	Supplies
Opener (Option 1)	5 to 10	**Cake of Dreams**—Decorate a cake, then eat only one bite.	Cake, icing, cake decorations, knives
(Option 2)		**Baseball Trivia**—Take a trivia test to learn about Dave Dravecky's life.	"Baseball Trivia" handouts (p. 40), pencils
Action and Reflection	10 to 15	**Capture the Dream**—Play a game representing the pursuit of a dream.	Toothpicks, masking tape, red and blue markers
Bible Application	15 to 20	**Good Results**—Present their dreams to be judged and read about Job's response to suffering.	Bibles
Commitment	5 to 10	**Sweet Dreams**—Affirm God's dreams for each other.	Cake from "Cake of Dreams" activity or doughnuts
Closing (Option 1)	up to 5	**The Dream Team**—Share their dreams for the class.	Newsprint, markers
(Option 2)		**Thanks for Sharing**—Write a letter to the Dave Dravecky Foundation.	Paper, pencils or pens

The Lesson

OPENER
(5 to 10 minutes)

☐ OPTION 1: CAKE OF DREAMS

Before class, bake or buy a sheet cake for students to decorate. Bring the cake to class along with icing, any other decorations you want, and knives for spreading the icing. Keep the cake covered where students won't see it.

Say: **I want you to close your eyes and imagine the perfect cake. Maybe it's a birthday cake you had when you were little; maybe it's a cake you've seen in a bakery and always wanted to taste.**

While students have their eyes closed, bring out the cake you've brought. Invite students to open their eyes.

Say: **I know this cake isn't perfect, but I've brought some icing and decorations for it. Let's all work together to make the best cake we can.**

Let students take their time decorating the cake to make it as elaborate as they can with the supplies you've brought. After they've finished decorating the cake, cut it into normal-sized slices. Then cut two or three of the slices into small, bite-sized pieces and give each person only one bite. Put the rest of the cake away.

Ask:

● **How did our finished cake compare to your dream cakes?** (It wasn't as fancy; I couldn't tell from only one bite.)

● **How is tasting one bite of a cake you've worked hard to make like achieving a dream and then losing it?** (You just begin to know what it's like, then you lose it; you look forward to something, then it's gone; you feel like all your hard work was wasted.)

Say: **Dave Dravecky began to dream of playing professional baseball when he was 7 years old. His dream became a reality when he was drafted by the Pittsburgh Pirates. After several years of hard work and a couple of trades, Dave Dravecky pitched for the San Diego Padres in the 1984 World Series. But just as Dave was tasting the sweet success of his dream, a cancerous lump was discovered in his pitching arm. The lump forced him to retire from baseball, and eventually his arm had to be amputated at the shoulder. Today we'll see what lessons we can learn from Dave about pursuing dreams and dealing with disappointment.**

☐ OPTION 2: BASEBALL TRIVIA

Before class, photocopy the "Baseball Trivia" handout (p. 40).

Say: **We're going to be studying the example of Dave Dravecky today, so I thought a little baseball trivia might help get us in the mood.**

Distribute copies of the handout and pencils to students. Give them a few minutes to complete the handout, then read the correct answers:

1. False. The San Diego Padres traded Dave to the San Francisco Giants in 1987.

2. True. He was celebrating winning the National League championship with his teammates on the field.

3. True. His cancer doctor's assistant played for the Cincinnati Bengals.

4. False. Dave played two seasons of winter ball in Baranquilla, Columbia.

5. True.

6. False. Dave earned only $600 to 700 per month when he played in Columbia.

7. True.

8. True. Dave returned to the minor leagues to slowly work back into shape after having surgery on his pitching arm.

9. False. Dave retired because he lost the use of his pitching arm.

Say: **Dave Dravecky spent nearly 30 years of his life pursuing his dream of professional baseball. Then after one brief doctor's appointment, his dream was crushed. Today we're going to learn about**

Teacher Tip

If students are unfamiliar with Dave Dravecky, take a moment to read aloud the biographical information about him in the introduction to this course (p. 5).

Dave Dravecky's life and how God's dreams for us may sometimes be different from our own dreams.

CAPTURE THE DREAM

Before the meeting prepare an even number of "flags" using toothpicks and masking tape. (You'll need one flag for each student.) Tear a piece of tape approximately 2 inches long and fold it in half around the toothpick. Make a blue X on half the flags, and a red X on the others.

Form two teams of equal size. One team will have red flags; the other, blue. Set a chair for each team on opposite sides of the room. Tape a masking tape line down the center of the room.

Give each person a toothpick flag to place on his or her team's chair. Have teams each appoint a "catcher" to stand near the chair to guard their flags from the other team.

Say: **This game is played like Capture the Flag, but with miniature flags. The object is to see which team can get more of the other team's flags back to its chair.**

Once you steal a flag from the other team, that team can block you or tag you. You must hold the flag in the air so everyone can see it, and each time you're tagged, you must hold up a finger. If you're tagged three times, you're out. Just like in baseball. I'll be the umpire and call you out if I see you holding up three fingers. We'll play nine 30-second innings. Ready? Go.

Monitor the progress of the game and call time after each "inning." After each inning, team members must return to their own side of the tape. They can keep holding flags they've taken, and the number of fingers they're holding up should stay the same. After you've played all nine innings, ask:

● **What obstacles did you face as you tried to capture the other team's flags?** (I had to maneuver my way through the other team; I had to get past the catcher; I had to hold on to the flag and not drop it.)

● **What were you thinking as you fought your way through the other team to their chair?** (I was hoping I'd make it through; I was excited because I wanted to score points for my team; I was concentrating on steering my way around three people.)

● **How did you react as you were tagged after you captured a flag?** (I felt pretty safe because I still had two more "strikes;" I worried I wouldn't make it to my team's chair.)

● **How is trying to capture the other team's flags like pursuing a dream in life?** (We had to face obstacles before we could get the flags; once we got the flags we weren't guaranteed we'd get to keep them.)

Say: **Sometimes obstacles stand in the way of our dreams; other times we capture our dreams, then lose them like Dave Dravecky did with his dream of**

ACTION AND REFLECTION
(10 to 15 minutes)

professional baseball. But whether or not we attain our dreams, God can help guide our dreams. Let's identify some of our dreams now.

GOOD RESULTS

Form pairs. Give kids two or three minutes to think of a dream that's been important to them and share it with their partners.

Say: **I hereby declare this court to be in session. I am the judge and jury. Please step up and defend your partner's dream to me.**

After each dream is presented, pretend to consult a large Bible or dictionary. Answer each request arbitrarily with one of the following responses: "Surely you've sinned. Your dream is denied." "You don't have enough faith. Your dream is denied." "Your dream is denied. Denial grows character."

After you've denied all the requests, ask:

● **How did you feel when your dream was denied? Explain.** (Angry, because it was a perfectly good dream; confused, because I didn't understand the reason you gave me.)

● **How satisfying were the explanations I gave you? Explain.** (Satisfying, I know I don't have as much faith as I should; unsatisfying, I think I have plenty of character already; I don't think God keeps us from our dreams if we aren't perfect.)

Say: **A man in the Bible, Job, received some of these same explanations for his problems and found them very unsatisfying. Job's loss was greater than a dream—he lost his family, all he owned, and nearly lost his life. His friends offered him plenty of advice. Let's read some of it.**

Have students form two circles, one within the other. Have team A's members form the inner circle and face outward. Have team B's members form the outer circle and face inward.

Ask three volunteers to read Job 8:4-6; 11:14; and 15:11-13 aloud. Have kids pair up with the person in front of them and answer the following question.

● **How would you feel if you were Job and you heard those arguments from your friends?** (I'd be mad at my friends for arguing with me instead of taking care of me; I wouldn't understand why my friends weren't on my side.)

Next, tell kids in the outer circle to rotate one space to the right and form new pairs to discuss the next question. Repeat this process for each remaining question.

● **Do you think any good could come out of Job's suffering? Why or why not?** (He might learn something; I doubt it, he'd probably become hard and angry.)

● **Do you think any good could come from Dave Dravecky's suffering? Why or why not?** (Maybe God had something else in mind for Dave Dravecky besides baseball;

I'd think he'd be really frustrated and mad at God.)

Have kids remain in the circles and say: **In his book, *When You Can't Come Back,* Dave Dravecky distinguishes between the purpose and result of suffering. After surgery, his doctor said Dave's amputated arm was sent immediately to the pathology department for research. As a *result*, doctors used his arm to learn more about Dave's type of cancer. But it would have been wrong if the *purpose* for Dave's amputation was to obtain a research specimen. Doctors can't just go around chopping off healthy arms to do cancer research. Let's read what the Bible has to say about the results of our suffering.**

Read Romans 5:1-5 aloud. Have students continue to rotate and find new discussion partners with each new question.

Ask:

● **According to these verses, what are the results of our suffering?** (Patience; hope; God's comfort through the Holy Spirit.)

● **Think about the dream you shared with your partner earlier. Could any good result from the loss of that dream?** (Answers will vary.)

Say: **Because Dave Dravecky lost his pitching arm, he was forced to retire from baseball. But as a result, he's been able to touch many lives for Christ with his story and his calm determination to live a happy, fulfilled life without baseball.**

COMMITMENT
(5 to 10 minutes)

SWEET DREAMS

If you used the "Cake of Dreams" option as an opener, bring the remaining cake out. If not, use doughnuts for this activity.

Ask:

● **What do you think God's dreams are for you?** (To tell others about Christ; to love others; to be a good example to others.)

● **How is God acting in your life to make these dreams reality?** (By giving me Christian friends; God is using this class to help me grow; God has given me challenging situations to make me stronger.)

Have each person take a piece of cake (or a doughnut).

Say: **Think of others in this class who God is using to help you become more like God. Maybe someone here has prayed for you or encouraged you in a rough time. Move about the room and give these people a piece of your cake as you thank them for what they're doing.**

When students have done this, say: **God's dreams for Dave Dravecky and Dave's dreams for himself were different. Let's remember to pursue God's dreams for us as well as our own dreams.**

OPTION 1: THE DREAM TEAM

Brainstorm "dream ideas" for your class. For example, students might want to make a commitment to take a missions trip, bring more friends to meetings, or grow closer to one another. Then form groups of no more than four. Give each group a sheet of newsprint and a marker. Have each group create an action plan for one of the ideas. These plans should list specific actions class members can take to make their dream a reality.

Have each group share its action plan. As a group, decide on at least one action plan to begin working on in the next week.

Close in prayer, asking God to help students strive for God's dreams above their own.

OPTION 2: THANKS FOR SHARING

Have students write letters to the Dave Dravecky Foundation expressing their appreciation to Dave for sharing his inspiring story. You may write to the foundation at this address:

The Dave Dravecky Foundation
Box 3505
Boardman, Ohio 44513

Close in prayer, thanking God for using others as inspiration to keep going even when dreams don't come true.

CLOSING
(up to 5 minutes)

If You Still Have Time . . .

Count Your Blessings—Have kids brainstorm a list of unfair experiences they've had. Then have them list one or more blessings God has given them for each unfair experience they listed. For example, not getting to go to camp because of the cost could be an unfair experience. Making a new friend with another student who couldn't go could be a resulting blessing.

Which list is longer? Why?

Lean on Me—Form pairs and have students look up Proverbs 3:5-6. Play this simple game to remind kids what happens when they "lean" on their own understanding.

Have students stand with both feet together on the ground and lean as far as possible to the right. See who can lean the farthest without falling. Then have kids lean against their partners' backs.

Discuss which was easier: leaning on a partner or leaning on their own ability. How is this like leaning on God instead of ourselves?

BASEBALL TRIVIA

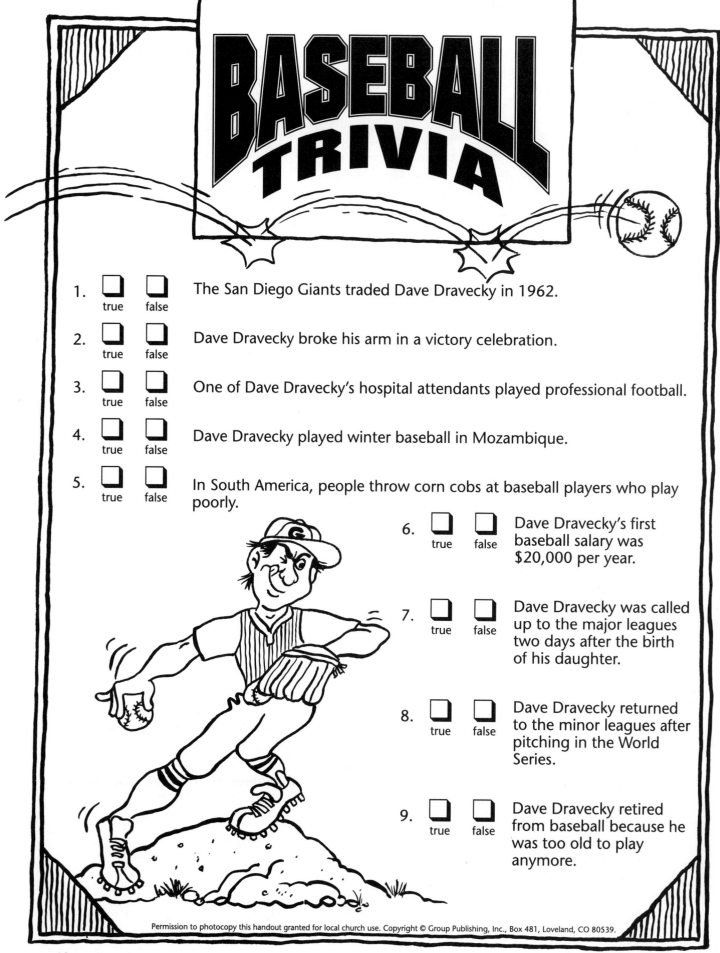

1. ☐ true ☐ false — The San Diego Giants traded Dave Dravecky in 1962.

2. ☐ true ☐ false — Dave Dravecky broke his arm in a victory celebration.

3. ☐ true ☐ false — One of Dave Dravecky's hospital attendants played professional football.

4. ☐ true ☐ false — Dave Dravecky played winter baseball in Mozambique.

5. ☐ true ☐ false — In South America, people throw corn cobs at baseball players who play poorly.

6. ☐ true ☐ false — Dave Dravecky's first baseball salary was $20,000 per year.

7. ☐ true ☐ false — Dave Dravecky was called up to the major leagues two days after the birth of his daughter.

8. ☐ true ☐ false — Dave Dravecky returned to the minor leagues after pitching in the World Series.

9. ☐ true ☐ false — Dave Dravecky retired from baseball because he was too old to play anymore.

OUT OF CONTROL: TERRY ANDERSON

One March day in Lebanon, Associated Press reporter Terry Anderson arranged to meet a friend for a game of tennis. He had no idea he wouldn't see another tennis racket for nearly seven years. Terry Anderson was kidnapped March 16, 1985, shortly after his tennis game.

For 2,455 days, terrorists held Anderson hostage. Early in his captivity, Anderson joined with other hostages in holding simple worship services. He maintained hope during those long days by reading his Bible.

This lesson will use Terry Anderson's example to help students hold on to their faith, even when circumstances are out of their control.

To help senior highers trust God when their lives seem out of control.

LESSON AIM

Students will
- **experience frustrations of circumstances beyond their control,**
- **learn how Bible characters handled situations they couldn't control, and**
- **affirm that God is in control of their lives.**

OBJECTIVES

Look up the following Scriptures. Then read the background paragraphs to see how the passages relate to your senior highers.

Daniel 1:1-16; 2:1-23, 48-49; 3:4-30; and **6:1-28** relate the experiences of Daniel and his friends while they were captives in Babylon.

Daniel and his friends lost control over their circumstances when King Nebuchadnezzar invaded Judah. As captives in Babylon, they were expected to conform to Babylonian customs, including worshiping the Babylonian gods. By encouraging each other and praying for deliverance, Daniel and his friends managed to survive their captivity.

Teenagers often find themselves losing control of their lives. Their parents may divorce; they may be forced to move to a new school; they may feel they've been treated unfairly by a teacher or classmate. The example of the young men in these passages will show teenagers ways to reach out to God and others so they can persevere in spite of difficult circumstances.

Romans 8:28-31 promises that if we trust God, God will bring good out of difficult circumstances.

Paul probably faced more difficult circumstances in the course of his ministry than any teenager or adult today will ever face. So when Paul wrote that God works for the good of those who love him, he wasn't just theorizing. He lived that promise and shared it with the church as a proven fact.

It's difficult for teenagers to trust their circumstances to God. They're quickly becoming adults and desperately want to exercise their new-found independence by grasping control of their lives. Kids need to realize that God can guide them through circumstances that are beyond their control.

Section	Minutes	What Students Will Do	Supplies
Opener (Option 1)	5 to 10	**Where Were You?**—Try to remember where they were on specific dates.	Chalkboard, chalk
(Option 2)		**Plot Your Life**—Draw time lines of the next six years of their lives.	Newsprint, tape, markers
Action and Reflection	10 to 15	**Silent Search**—Play a game of silent Hide-and-Seek while blindfolded.	Blindfolds
Bible Application	15 to 20	**Survival Strategies**—Learn about survivors of the Babylonian captivity by doing circuit training.	"Survival Circuit-Training" handouts (p. 49), vegetables, Bibles
Commitment	5 to 10	**Held Hostage**—Form a human cage and affirm God's control of their circumstances through prayer.	Bible
Closing (Option 1)	up to 5	**Prayer Alert**—Pray for captives around the world.	
(Option 2)		**Singing to Safety**—Choose a favorite song to sing when life gets out of control.	Hymnals or chorus books

The Lesson

☐ OPTION 1: WHERE WERE YOU?

Form two groups: the witnesses and the interrogators. On the chalkboard write, "Where were you on March 16?"

Say: **Interrogators, you have one minute to ask this question to as many witnesses as possible. Witnesses, you must answer the question as well as your memories allow.**

After a minute, call time. Then switch roles. Have the new interrogators ask the new witnesses the same question, but with a slight variation: "Where were you on March 16 one year ago?"

Continue switching roles and going back in time until you run out of time or go back to 1985, whichever comes first. After kids have completed the activity, ask:

● **What were you thinking as you tried to remember where you were each March 16?** (I didn't understand the importance of March 16; I wished I had a better memory because it got harder to remember as we went back in time.)

● **What makes it hard to remember what you were doing on a specific day?** (It's hard to remember things from a long time ago; I don't always do the same thing every day; March 16 isn't a holiday or special day for me.)

OPENER
(5 to 10 minutes)

Say: **For Terry Anderson and his family, March 16, 1985, was a day that changed their lives. On that day, Terry was taken hostage in Lebanon and held until December 5, 1991. Terry's faith in God helped him maintain hope even though the situation was completely out of his control. Today we're going to see how we can follow Terry Anderson's example when we find ourselves in situations we can't control.**

☐ OPTION 2: PLOT YOUR LIFE

Before class, tape sheets of newsprint at eye level around the room. (You'll need one newsprint sheet for each student.) Place a marker on the floor under each sheet of newsprint.

As students arrive, have each one stand by a sheet of newsprint.

Say: **Beginning with today, draw a time line mapping out your life for the next six years. Be sure to include any important items such as birthdays, upcoming graduations, or personal goals on your time lines.**

Give students about three minutes to complete their time lines, then call the class back together.

Say: **Imagine that your life as you've just planned it ceased to exist for the next six years.**

Walk around the room and draw a large X over each of the time lines. Then have students form trios and discuss the following questions. Pause after you ask each question to allow groups time for discussion.

● **How did you react as I crossed out all the plans you made?** (I was annoyed; I felt confused.)

● **How is this like the way you'd feel if you suddenly found out you couldn't do anything you'd planned for several years? Explain.** (Similar, I'd be disappointed because I was looking forward to going to college; angry that I didn't have any control over the situation; I'd feel much worse if I really couldn't do anything I've planned.)

● **What major events in your family might you miss if you disappeared for the next six years?** (My sister's graduation; my brother's wedding; lots of birthdays and vacations.)

Say: **Terry Anderson was held hostage in Lebanon for six years. He missed his daughter's birth and the first six years of her life, as well as countless other important occasions. Today we're going to look at Terry's example to learn ways to handle situations that are out of our control.**

Teacher Tip

If students are unfamiliar with Terry Anderson, take a moment to read the biographical information about him in the introduction to this course (p. 6).

SILENT SEARCH

Say: **Let's play a simple game of Hide-and-Seek. Find a partner and decide who will hide and who will seek. I'll step outside the door with the seekers for a minute or two while the hiders hide as well as they can in this room.**

Lead the seekers outside the door and blindfold them.

Say: **You must look for your partners while crawling on your hands and knees. You may not talk to each other or to your partners at any time. If you bump into another seeker you may crawl with that person, but remember to remain silent.**

As you lead the seekers back into the room, put your finger to your lips to signal the hiders to keep quiet. Have the seekers crawl around, hunting for their partners. After two minutes allow hiders to call out their partners' names once as a clue. The first pair to find each other wins. Continue having hiders call out their partners' names at one-minute intervals until each seeker has found his or her partner. Allow seekers to remove their blindfolds.

Have kids stand as you ask the following questions. When one student shares an answer, anyone who agrees with that answer and has nothing more to add may sit down. When all kids are seated, ask the next question and repeat the process.

● **How did you feel when you discovered the seekers were to be blindfolded?** (Depressed because I didn't know how my partner would ever find me; cheated, if I'd known I was going to be blindfolded I wouldn't have volunteered to be a seeker.)

● **Hiders, describe how you felt when you couldn't help your partners.** (Angry; frustrated; hopeless.)

● **Seekers, how did you respond when you bumped into another seeker?** (I was comforted to know I wasn't the only one still looking; happy to have someone to crawl around with.)

● **During the early part of his captivity, Terry Anderson shared a cell with several other hostages. How are the feelings you've just described like the feelings Terry Anderson and the other hostages might have had in captivity?** (They were probably glad to have some company, at least; they might have been frustrated that they couldn't help one another escape.)

● **Hiders, what was your reaction when you got to call your partners' names?** (I thought we might have a chance after all; I was relieved to finally be able to help.)

● **Seekers, how did you feel when you heard your names?** (Glad to know which direction to crawl; relieved to have some help.)

● **How are these feelings like the feelings Terry**

ACTION AND REFLECTION
(10 to 15 minutes)

Teacher Tip

If all kids sit down after the first student shares an answer, have kids stand up and ask the question again to encourage another response.

Anderson and his fellow hostages might have had when they were freed? (They were relieved their ordeal was over; they were glad to be able to see and talk and move around normally again.)

Say: **Just like you called out to your partners as they were about to give up, Terry Anderson and his fellow hostages kept hope alive during their captivity by reaching out to one another. As often as they were allowed, they met for prayer and worship together. Let's see how some prisoners in the Bible handled captivity.**

BIBLE APPLICATION
(15 to 20 minutes)

SURVIVAL STRATEGIES

You'll need a plate of raw vegetables, such as carrot sticks, for this activity. Photocopy the "Survival Circuit-Training" handout (p. 49). Cut the handout apart and post the instructions for each station on separate walls. Place the plate of vegetables on a table beside the station 1 instructions. Put a Bible near each station.

Form teams of no more than four.

Say: **Terry Anderson and his fellow hostages kept from getting too bored or sick during their captivity by exercising in their cells. I've set up a short circuit-training course in the room today. The instructions posted at each station include a Scripture for your team to read and discuss as well as a physical exercise to perform. You'll have about 10 minutes. Complete as many stations as you can in the time allowed.**

Start each team at a different station. (If your class is large, two or more teams may work at the same station at the same time, provided they work as separate teams.) Give teams about 10 minutes to complete as many stations as possible, then call time. Teams probably won't be able to complete all four stations, but each team will have completed at least one.

Ask teams to summarize for the whole class the stories they read at their stations. Then have students share the strategies for dealing with out-of-control circumstances they learned from Daniel and his friends. After all teams have shared, discuss the following questions:

● **How do you think Daniel and his friends felt in the out-of-control situations you read about?** (Confused about the customs of a strange place; afraid they'd be tortured or killed for their faith in God; confident that God would protect them if they followed God.)

● **How would you feel if you were in a similar situation?** (Afraid I was going to die; glad to have a few friends around; nervous that I'd make the king mad.)

● **What strategy could you use this week when you feel like circumstances are out of your control?** (I could pray for God to show me what to do when I have to make a tough decision; I could tell my friends what I'm going through and ask for their support.)

Say: **Terry Anderson and his fellow hostages used some of these same strategies to survive their captivity in Lebanon. If we rely on God and the encouragement of others, we can survive our out-of-control situations, too.**

HELD HOSTAGE

Say: **Even though we haven't been physically imprisoned and held against our will like Terry Anderson, we all encounter circumstances that are out of our control. Let's identify some of those circumstances now.**

Have kids stand and form a circle. Have students spread their feet apart so they're touching the feet of the people next to them. Have everyone raise their hands toward the center to form a human "cage."

Read Romans 8:28-31 aloud.

Say: **Even though at times it may not seem like it, God is always in control. As you step into this "cage" one at a time, name a circumstance you're affected by but can't control.**

For example, maybe your parents are getting a divorce, or your boyfriend or girlfriend wants to break up with you. After you've shared your out-of-control circumstance, the person who stands to your left in the "cage" will say a short prayer, thanking God for you and asking God to give you strength in your situation.

Tell kids they don't have to go into great detail about the situation if they don't feel comfortable doing so. Select one student to go first and begin the activity. Repeat the activity until each student has been encouraged through prayer.

☐ OPTION 1: PRAYER ALERT

Ask:

● **There are hostages and prisoners held throughout the world because of wars and religious or political conflicts. How do you think you'd react in a hostage's situation?** (I'd be angry for a long time; I'd give up; I'd do my best to escape.)

● **How do you react when out-of-control situations in life seem to take you hostage?** (I hide in my room and sleep; I get angry and take it out on others; I work harder to fix the situation.)

Say: **We may not be able to free captives or change situations out of our control, but God can help anyone held hostage by circumstances.**

Have kids close in prayer, asking God to bring hope, encouragement, and strength to captives of all kinds and their families around the world.

COMMITMENT
(5 to 10 minutes)

Teacher Tip
If your class has more than 10 members, form two or more "cages."

CLOSING
(up to 5 minutes)

Note: Depending on the world situation at the time you lead this lesson, you may know the names of specific hostages or prisoners. For example, missionaries may be held by terrorists, or Americans might be held in other countries. Have students write letters to the families of these captives. Tell the families that you're praying for them and their loved ones and that you hope for a swift and safe release.

Families of missionaries may be reached through missions organizations. Letters to families of Americans held captive may be sent in care of the Department of State in Washington, D.C. To find out where to direct your letter, call the State Department at (202) 647-4000.

☐ OPTION 2: SINGING TO SAFETY

Collect four or five hymnals or chorus books. Form groups and give each group a hymnal or chorus book. Have each group select a song that talks about trusting God and summarize its message.

Have groups share their songs' messages. If your class knows any of the songs, sing as many as time allows.

Close by singing the most familiar song as a prayer.

If You Still Have Time . . .

Get a Grip—Have kids pantomime situations that cause them to feel out of control. These can be funny or serious. For example, they might feel out of control while taking a driver's license exam, or when asking someone out on a date. After other kids have correctly guessed the pantomime, have them offer suggestions for gaining more control in that situation.

Course Reflection—Form pairs. Have kids interview their partners about what they've learned during the past four weeks. Encourage teenagers to ask questions such as:

● What's something new you learned during this course?
● What have you done differently since this course began?
● How will you apply what you've learned to your everyday life?

After about five minutes, have volunteers share with the whole class the answers their partners gave.

Survival Circuit-Training

Station 1

1. Read Daniel 1:1-16 together and summarize the story in your own words.

2. Eat a vegetable from the plate, then do five sit-ups to help speed digestion.

3. As a team, determine what Daniel's strategy for handling this out-of-control situation was.

Station 2

1. Read Daniel 2:1-23, 48-49 together and summarize the story in your own words.

2. Run in place for one minute to prepare to outrun the guards who'll tear you from limb to limb.

3. As a team, discuss what Daniel and his friends' strategy for handling this out-of-control situation was.

Station 3

1. Read Daniel 3:4-30 together and summarize the story in your own words.

2. Do 10 jumping jacks to keep your feet from touching the flames.

3. What did Shadrach, Meshach, and Abednego do to handle this situation?

Station 4

1. Read Daniel 6:1-28 together and summarize the story in your own words.

2. Do 10 knee bends as you're kneeling to pray.

3. What was Daniel's strategy for handling this out-of-control situation?

BONUS IDEAS

Bonus Scriptures— The lessons focus on a few selected Scripture passages, but if you'd like to incorporate more Bible readings into the lesson, here are some suggestions:
- 1 Samuel 17:1-51 (David fights Goliath.)
- Esther (Esther risks her life to save her people.)
- Habakkuk 1:1-4 (Habakkuk is frustrated with a world that's out of control.)
- Matthew 2:1-11 (Wise men worship our true hero, Jesus.)
- Acts 4:8-18 (Great Christians shouldn't be worshiped.)
- 1 Corinthians 1:10-17 (We should follow God, not heroes.)

Bonus Books— For students in your group who want to know more about the heroes and situations you've covered in the course, recommend the following resources:

"Amy Grant— Leading the Way," by Devlin Donaldson in *The Heart of the Matter: The CCM Interviews Volume 1.* Nashville: Star Song Communications, 1991, p. 45.

"Amy's Heart in Motion," by Julie A. Talerico in Today's Christian Woman, November–December 1992, p. 54.

Joni by Joni Eareckson. Grand Rapids: Zondervan, 1976.

A Step Further by Joni Eareckson Tada and Steve Estes. Grand Rapids: Zondervan, 1978.

Comeback by Dave Dravecky. New York: Harper Collins, 1990.

When You Can't Come Back by Dave and Jan Dravecky. Grand Rapids: Zondervan, 1992.

Hostage Freed by Eric Jacobsen. Elgin: David C. Cook, 1991.

What's It Really Like?— Call ahead and schedule a visit to a local residential treatment facility for the physically challenged. Ask if there are any residents who would be willing to speak to your class about what it's really like to be disabled. Talk about the visit before you go and prepare students to share their own weaknesses as well.

The Dream Team— Rent video footage from the 1992 U.S. Olympic basketball team (available in most video stores). Watch as much of the video as your group is interested in, then discuss the phenomenon of the "sports hero." Discuss reasons so many athletes associate dreams with their sport and talk about athletes who have fallen short of their dreams because of drug abuse, involvement in crime, sickness, injury, or other reasons.

Who's Your Hero?— Lead kids on an interview scavenger hunt around the church after a Sunday morning or midweek service. Have members of your class take turns asking people of various ages about their heroes. If you have access to a video camera you can tape the interviews; otherwise, have kids jot down notes and share their results at the next meeting. Encourage kids to ask the following people who their heroes are and why:

- a 3-year-old boy,
- a 3-year-old girl,
- a third-grade girl,
- a third-grade boy, and

ask the following people who their heroes are and if they're the same heroes they had in the past:

- a seventh-grade boy,
- a seventh-grade girl,
- a youth group member of the same sex,
- a youth group member of the opposite sex,
- parents of youth group members, and
- grandparents of youth group members or other older people in the church.

You're My Hero— Have kids write letters of appreciation to their heroes explaining why they admire them. Appoint one or two kids to research addresses and fan clubs for the heroes selected by your class.

Rise and Fall of the American Hero— Play "Hero" from Steve Taylor's *Meltdown* album. Discuss the song, then brainstorm a list of "worldly" heroes and a list of Christian heroes. Form pairs and give each pair one hero from each list. Have pairs compare and contrast the qualities their heroes exhibit, then present their responses to the class. Based on the presentations, vote on the list of heroes and add or subtract names as necessary. Have students design an "Our Heroes" poster to post in the classroom.

Mentor Match— Match kids with adult volunteers from your congregation. Ask that partners spend an hour or more together each month, call each other weekly, and pray for each other daily. An adult willing to help a teenager grow is a true hero!

Table Talk— Use the "Table Talk" handout (p. 22) as the basis for a meeting with the kids and their parents. During the meeting, have the parents and kids complete the handout and discuss it.

Present several famous past and present heroes and allow kids and parents to evaluate the heroic qualities of these people. Discuss what makes a hero and how it might feel to be one.

PARTY PLEASERS

Hero Party— Invite kids to come to a party dressed as their favorite Bible or modern hero. Serve hero sandwiches and watch old *Batman* or *Superman* TV episodes (available at most video stores).

Locked in Lock-In— Have an overnight lock-in at the church or a group member's house. As students arrive, assign each one a disability that he or she must live with for the next several hours. For example, blindfold some students; instruct a few not to speak; for some, restrict the use various limbs; and so on. If possible, have several adult volunteers serve as "disability patrol" to make sure students are living with their disabilities at all times. Play your usual lock-in games and let students get a better feel for what it's like to be disabled.

RETREAT IDEA

Superheroes— Have a retreat on the theme of heroes.
Have students form teams for the entire event and name themselves after a superhero. Possible team names could be Batman's Brigade, Wonder Woman's Winners, or Superman's Super Team.
Try these superhero games:
● Muscle Maker— Teams try to fit as many balloons into their clothing as possible to make fake muscles.
● I Yam What I Yam— The team able to consume the most canned spinach in one minute wins the Popeye award.
● Power Ball— This game is played like softball, but each team member has a different heroic ability he or she must always display. For example, one person may be able to fly, so team members will have to carry this person in a flying position during all runs. Another person may be invisible and have to say, "Here I am! Here I am!" continually so team members can see him or her. Another player may be able to leap over buildings, so must leap everywhere. If you run out of ideas for heroic qualities, have the kids help you think of more!
Plan devotions on the concept of Jesus as the real superhero. Focus sessions on various qualities of Jesus that make him a hero. For example, Jesus had compassion for the poor and weak, Jesus fought against evil, and Jesus displayed great power.

CURRICULUM REORDER—TOP PRIORITY

Order now to prepare for your upcoming Sunday school classes, youth ministry meetings, and weekend retreats! Each book includes all teacher and student materials—plus photo-copiable handouts—for any size class...for just $8.99 each!

FOR SENIOR HIGH:

1 & 2 Corinthians: Christian Discipleship, ISBN 1-55945-230-7

Angels, Demons, Miracles & Prayer, ISBN 1-55945-235-8

Changing the World, ISBN 1-55945-236-6

Christians in a Non-Christian World, ISBN 1-55945-224-2

Christlike Leadership, ISBN 1-55945-231-5

Communicating With Friends, ISBN 1-55945-228-5

Counterfeit Religions, ISBN 1-55945-207-2

Dating Decisions, ISBN 1-55945-215-3

Dealing With Life's Pressures, ISBN 1-55945-232-3

Deciphering Jesus' Parables, ISBN 1-55945-237-4

Exodus: Following God, ISBN 1-55945-226-9

Exploring Ethical Issues, ISBN 1-55945-225-0

Faith for Tough Times, ISBN 1-55945-216-1

Forgiveness, ISBN 1-55945-223-4

Getting Along With Parents, ISBN 1-55945-202-1

Getting Along With Your Family, ISBN 1-55945-233-1

The Gospel of John: Jesus' Teachings, ISBN 1-55945-208-0

Hazardous to Your Health: AIDS, Steroids & Eating Disorders, ISBN 1-55945-200-5

Is Marriage in Your Future?, ISBN 1-55945-203-X

Jesus' Death & Resurrection, ISBN 1-55945-211-0

The Joy of Serving, ISBN 1-55945-210-2

Knowing God's Will, ISBN 1-55945-205-6

Life After High School, ISBN 1-55945-220-X

Making Good Decisions, ISBN 1-55945-209-9

Money: A Christian Perspective, ISBN 1-55945-212-9

Movies, Music, TV & Me, ISBN 1-55945-213-7

Overcoming Insecurities, ISBN 1-55945-221-8

Psalms, ISBN 1-55945-234-X

Real People, Real Faith: Amy Grant, Joni Eareckson Tada, Dave Dravecky, Terry Anderson, ISBN 1-55945-238-2

Responding to Injustice, ISBN 1-55945-214-5

Revelation, ISBN 1-55945-229-3

School Struggles, ISBN 1-55945-201-3

Sex: A Christian Perspective, ISBN 1-55945-206-4

Today's Lessons From Yesterday's Prophets, ISBN 1-55945-227-7

Turning Depression Upside Down, ISBN 1-55945-135-1

What Is the Church?, ISBN 1-55945-222-6

Who Is God?, ISBN 1-55945-218-8

Who Is Jesus?, ISBN 1-55945-219-6

Who Is the Holy Spirit?, ISBN 1-55945-217-X

Your Life as a Disciple, ISBN 1-55945-204-8

FOR JUNIOR HIGH/MIDDLE SCHOOL:

Accepting Others: Beyond Barriers & Stereotypes, ISBN 1-55945-126-2

Advice to Young Christians: Exploring Paul's Letters, ISBN 1-55945-146-7

Applying the Bible to Life, ISBN 1-55945-116-5

Becoming Responsible, ISBN 1-55945-109-2

Bible Heroes: Joseph, Esther, Mary & Peter, ISBN 1-55945-137-8

Boosting Self-Esteem, ISBN 1-55945-100-9

Building Better Friendships, ISBN 1-55945-138-6

Can Christians Have Fun?, ISBN 1-55945-134-3

Caring for God's Creation, ISBN 1-55945-121-1

Christmas: A Fresh Look, ISBN 1-55945-124-6

Competition, ISBN 1-55945-133-5

Dealing With Death, ISBN 1-55945-112-2

Dealing With Disappointment, ISBN 1-55945-139-4

Doing Your Best, ISBN 1-55945-142-4

Drugs & Drinking, ISBN 1-55945-118-1

Evil and the Occult, ISBN 1-55945-102-5

Genesis: The Beginnings, ISBN 1-55945-111-4

Guys & Girls: Understanding Each Other, ISBN 1-55945-110-6

Handling Conflict, ISBN 1-55945-125-4

Heaven & Hell, ISBN 1-55945-131-9

Is God Unfair?, ISBN 1-55945-108-4

Love or Infatuation?, ISBN 1-55945-128-9

Making Parents Proud, ISBN 1-55945-107-6

Making the Most of School, ISBN 1-55945-113-0

Materialism, ISBN 1-55945-130-0

The Miracle of Easter, ISBN 1-55945-143-2

Miracles!, ISBN 1-55945-117-3

Peace & War, ISBN 1-55945-123-8

Peer Pressure, ISBN 1-55945-103-3

Prayer, ISBN 1-55945-104-1

Reaching Out to a Hurting World, ISBN 1-55945-140-8

Sermon on the Mount, ISBN 1-55945-129-7

Suicide: The Silent Epidemic, ISBN 1-55945-145-9

Telling Your Friends About Christ, ISBN 1-55945-114-9

The Ten Commandments, ISBN 1-55945-127-0

Today's Faith Heroes: Madeline Manning Mims, Michael W. Smith, Mother Teresa, Bruce Olson, ISBN 1-55945-141-6

Today's Media: Choosing Wisely, ISBN 1-55945-144-0

Today's Music: Good or Bad?, ISBN 1-55945-101-7

What Is God's Purpose for Me?, ISBN 1-55945-132-7

What's a Christian?, ISBN 1-55945-105-X

Order today from your local Christian bookstore, or write: Group Publishing, Box 485, Loveland, CO 80539. For mail orders, please add postage/handling of $4 for orders up to $15, $5 for orders of $15.01+. Colorado residents add 3% sales tax.

BRING THE BIBLE TO LIFE FOR YOUR 5TH- AND 6TH-GRADERS WITH GROUP'S *HANDS-ON BIBLE CURRICULUM*®

Energize your kids with Active Learning!

Group's **Hands-On Bible Curriculum** will help you teach the Bible in a radical new way. It's based on Active Learning—the same teaching method Jesus used.

Research shows that we retain less than 10% of what we hear or read. *But we remember up to 90% of what we experience.* Your 5th- and 6th-graders will experience spiritual lessons and learn to apply them to their daily lives! And—they'll go home remembering what they've learned.

In each lesson, students will participate in exciting and memorable learning experiences using fascinating gadgets and gizmos you've not seen with any other curriculum. Your 5th- and 6th-graders will discover biblical truths and <u>remember</u> what they learn—because they're <u>doing</u> instead of just listening.

You'll save time and money too!

While students are learning more, you'll be working less—simply follow the quick and easy instructions in the Teachers Guide. You'll get tons of material for an energy-packed 35- to 60-minute lesson. And, if you have extra time, there's an arsenal of Bonus Ideas and Time Stuffers to keep kids occupied—and learning! Plus, you'll SAVE BIG over other curriculum programs that require you to buy expensive separate student books—all student handouts in Group's **Hands-On Bible Curriculum** are photocopiable!

In addition to the easy-to-use Teachers Guide, you'll get all the essential teaching materials you need in a ready-to-use Learning Lab®. No more running from store to store hunting for lesson materials—all the active-learning tools you need to teach 13 exciting Bible lessons to any size class are provided for you in the Learning Lab.

Challenging topics every 13 weeks keep your kids coming back!

Group's **Hands-On Bible Curriculum** covers topics that matter to your kids and teaches them the Bible with integrity. Every quarter you'll explore three meaningful Bible-based subjects. Switching topics every month keeps your 5th- and 6th-graders enthused and coming back for more. The full two-year program will help your kids...

• make God-pleasing decisions,
• recognize their God-given potential, and
• seek to grow as Christians.

Take the boredom out of Sunday school, children's church, and youth group for your 5th- and 6th-graders. Make your job easier and more rewarding with no-fail lessons that are ready in a flash. Order Group's **Hands-On Bible Curriculum** for your 5th- and 6th-graders today.

MORE CREATIVE RESOURCES FOR YOUR YOUTH MINISTRY

Do It! Active Learning in Youth Ministry
Thom and Joani Schultz

Discover the keys to teaching creative faith-building lessons that teenagers look forward to...and remember for a lifetime. You'll learn how to design simple, fun programs that will help your kids...
- build community,
- develop communication skills,
- relate better to others,
- experience what it's really like to be a Christian,

...and apply the Bible to their daily challenges. Plus, you'll get 24 ready-to-use active-learning exercises complete with debriefing questions and Bible application. For example, your kids will...
- learn the importance of teamwork and the value of each team member by juggling six different objects as a group,
- experience community and the importance of sharing their lives using a doughnut, and
- grow more sensitive to others' needs by acting out Matthew 25:31-46

...just to name a few. And the practical index of over 30 active-learning resources will make your planning easier.

ISBN 0-931529-94-8

Boredom Busters
Cindy S. Hansen

Packed with 84 low- and no-cost activities for kids of all ages, this book will help you turn any blah meeting into a blast! Keep your kids' attention by...
- playing human-size tick-tack-toe,
- organizing an orchestra without any instruments,
- deciphering a scrambled Scripture,
- batting a balloon through an obstacle course, and
- working together to lift a teammate over a net.

Don't let boredom keep your youth group from growing in faith. Keep them involved with **Boredom Busters**!

ISBN 0-931529-77-8

Ready-to-Go Meetings for Youth Ministry

Save yourself time and energy—planning meetings your teenagers will love. Each of the 70 meetings includes clear instructions and carefully constructed discussion questions to make planning simple. All you have to do is collect the supplies and go!

Meetings explore issues facing teenagers today in fun, creative ways. Topics include...
- coping with fear,
- appearances,
- appreciating parents,
- forgiveness,
- dating,
- learning to listen,
- gossip,
- friendship,
- drugs

...and dozens more that impact kids' lives.

With **Ready-to-Go Meetings for Youth Ministry**, your preparation is quick and easy. And your teenagers don't just hear the truth—they experience it!

ISBN 1-55945-168-8

Order today from your local Christian bookstore, or write: Group Publishing, Box 485, Loveland, CO 80539. For mail orders, please add postage/handling of $4 for orders up to $15, $5 for orders of $15.01+. Colorado residents add 3% sales tax.